THIS BOOK BELONGS TO

_____

_____

START DATE   _____ / _____ / _____

HE READS TRUTH

FOUNDERS

FOUNDER
Raechel Myers

CO-FOUNDER
Amanda Bible Williams

EXECUTIVE

CHIEF EXECUTIVE OFFICER
Ryan Myers

CHIEF OPERATING OFFICER
Mark D. Bullard

EDITORIAL

MANAGING EDITOR
Lindsey Jacobi, MDiv

PRODUCTION EDITOR
Hannah Little, MTS

ASSOCIATE EDITOR
Kayla De La Torre, MAT

COPY EDITOR
Becca Owens, MA

CREATIVE

SENIOR ART DIRECTOR
Annie Glover

DESIGN MANAGER
Kelsea Allen

DESIGNERS
Savannah Ault
Mackenzie Peters
Ashley Phillips

OPERATIONS

OPERATIONS DIRECTOR
Allison Sutton

OPERATIONS MANAGER
Mary Beth Steed

GROUP SALES AND
ENGAGEMENT SPECIALIST
Karson Speth

OPERATIONS ASSISTANT
Emily Andrews

MARKETING

GROWTH MARKETING MANAGERS
Katie Bevels
Blake Showalter

PRODUCT MARKETING MANAGER
Krista Squibb

CONTENT MARKETING STRATEGIST
Tameshia Williams, ThM

SOCIAL MEDIA SPECIALIST
Bella Ponce

MARKETING SPECIALIST
Bailey Majewski

COMMUNITY ENGAGEMENT

COMMUNITY ENGAGEMENT
MANAGER
Delaney Coleman

COMMUNITY ENGAGEMENT
SPECIALISTS
Cait Baggerman
Katy McKnight

SHIPPING

SHIPPING MANAGER
Marian Welch

FULFILLMENT LEAD
Kajsa Matheny

FULFILLMENT SPECIALISTS
Hannah Lamb
Kelsey Simpson

CONTRIBUTORS

SPECIAL THANKS
John Greco, MDiv
Jessica Lamb, MA
Kara Gause
Bailey Gillespie
Ellen Taylor
Jeremy Mitchell
Abbey Benson
Davis DeLisi

SUBSCRIPTION INQUIRIES
orders@hereadstruth.com

COLOPHON

This book was printed in Nashville, Tennessee, on 60# Lynx Opaque Text under the direction of He Reads Truth. Cover is 100# Cougar Opaque with a soft touch lamination.

COPYRIGHT

Research support provided by Logos Bible Software™. Learn more at logos.com.

PROMISES OF GOD

GOD'S PROMISES ARE
TRUE AND EXTENDED
TO US IN CHRIST, EVEN
WHEN WE DON'T FULLY
UNDERSTAND THEM.

W e've all made mistakes when it comes to reading, understanding, and putting our faith in God's promises. We can mistake statements of faithful endurance for promises of achievement and success, or we might misunderstand the full extent of Old Testament context and how to interpret its promises for modern day readers. We may expect God to keep the world's promises or misquote God's words to make them work in our favor.

And while we can really get it wrong sometimes, there is so much grace. Because the beautiful truth is that God's promises are true and extended to us in Christ, even when we don't fully understand them. God keeps His promises the way He always intended to, even when we complicate or misinterpret them.

This is why our team created this book. We've heard many wise people tell us God's promises are both true and plentiful, and we wanted to create a resource that not only lays them out plainly, but more importantly, teaches us how to read promises in Scripture with both clarity and assurance. This reading plan represents months of prayer, study, and discussion. And we really do believe that what we have assembled in these pages will not only serve you for three weeks as a man in the Word of God every day, but will equip you to read, understand, and believe the unshakable promises of God for a lifetime. These words will not slip, even when you do. They will not change, even if you do.

We pray these words offer you hope and an anchor, comfort and freedom. These promises are for you.

Read on.

THE HE READS TRUTH TEAM

WEEKLY TRUTH
DAY 21

Each He Reads Truth resource is thoughtfully and artfully designed to highlight the beauty, goodness, and truth of Scripture in a way that reflects the themes of each curated reading plan.

The typography chosen for this book is a quiet serif, displayed in a bold and striking fashion, to remind us that though we stand in awe of the indescribable goodness of God's promises, they were meant to inform and shape our everyday lives.

We chose photography that shows both moments of stillness and movement to symbolize the process of patiently waiting and the action of promises being fulfilled. These powerful images remind us of God's faithfulness.

HOW TO USE THIS BOOK

He Reads Truth is a community of men dedicated to reading the Word of God every day. In this **Promises of God** reading plan, we will understand how Jesus is the fulfillment of all God's promises, look at the ways God's promises inform our actions as believers, and let God's promises shape our hope in Christ.

READ & REFLECT

Your **Promises of God** book focuses primarily on Scripture, with added features to come alongside your time with God's Word.

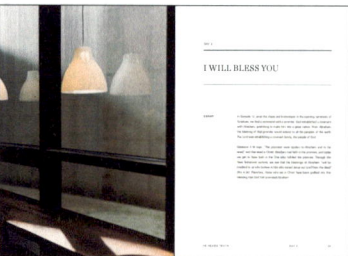

SCRIPTURE READING

Designed for a Monday start, this book presents daily readings on different promises of God.

PRAYER PROMPTS

Each weekday features a prompt for prayer.

COMMUNITY & CONVERSATION

You can start reading this book at any time. If you want to join men from across the globe as they read along with you, the He Reads Truth community will start Day 1 of **Promises of God** on Monday, February 10, 2025.

GRACE DAY

Use Saturdays to catch up on your reading, pray, and rest in the presence of the Lord.

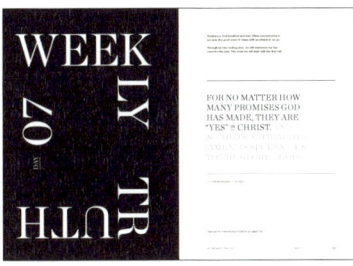

WEEKLY TRUTH

Sundays are set aside for Scripture memorization.

See tips for memorizing Scripture on page 124.

EXTRAS

This book features additional tools to help you gain a deeper understanding of the text.

Find a complete list of extras on page 10.

HE READS TRUTH APP

For added community and conversation, join us in the **Promises of God** reading plan on the He Reads Truth app. You can use the app to participate in community discussion and more.

HEREADSTRUTH.COM

The **Promises of God** reading plan will also be available at HeReadsTruth.com as the community reads each day. Invite your family, friends, and neighbors to read along with you.

TABLE OF CONTENTS

KEY VERSE

FOR NO MATTER HOW MANY PROMISES GOD HAS MADE, THEY ARE "YES" IN CHRIST. AND SO THROUGH HIM THE "AMEN" IS SPOKEN BY US TO THE GLORY OF GOD.

2 CORINTHIANS 1:20 NIV

HOW TO UNDERSTAND THE PROMISES OF GOD IN SCRIPTURE

The Bible is full of God's promises, and it tells us that "no matter how many promises God has made, they are 'Yes' in Christ" (2Co 1:20 NIV). But that doesn't mean we can apply every promise we read in Scripture directly to our lives today.

On the following pages are principles to help you better understand the promises of God. We've used God's promises to Abram (later Abraham) in Genesis 12 as an example to illustrate how these principles can be applied. As you move through each of the promises highlighted in this reading plan, feel free to return here for reminders as you go.

THE LORD SAID TO ABRAM:

Go out from your land,
your relatives,
and your father's house
to the land that I will show you.
I will make you into a great nation,
I will bless you,
I will make your name great,
and you will be a blessing.
I will bless those who bless you,
I will curse anyone who treats you with contempt,
and all the peoples on earth
will be blessed through you.

. . .

The LORD appeared to Abram and said, "To your offspring I will give this land." So he built an altar there to the LORD who had appeared to him.

GN 12:1–3, 7

GOD'S PROMISES WERE ORIGINALLY MADE to SPECIFIC PEOPLE in UNIQUE CIRCUMSTANCES.

Before considering if and how a promise might apply to us today, we should first understand how it was originally understood and applied.

God promised to make Abraham into a great nation and to bless him. This was first fulfilled as God grew the nation of Israel from Abraham's descendants.

SOME OF GOD'S PROMISES ARE CONDITIONAL.

All of God's promises depend solely on God, who is always faithful. However, some promises call for specific acts of human obedience.

God promised blessing for Abraham, but Abraham would have to leave his home and follow God to a land He would show him in order to see that promise fulfilled (Gn 12:1).

CONTEXT IS KEY TO DISCERNING THE EXTENT OF A PROMISE.

Oftentimes a promise from God will sound all-encompassing when taken from its original context, but further reading can clarify God's intent.

While God did indeed promise to make Abraham's name great, that greatness was always tied to Abraham's relationship with the Lord. As God worked through Abraham's life, the watching world's respect for Abraham and his God grew in tandem (Gn 14:19–20).

SOME PROMISES HAVE ALREADY BEEN FULFILLED, WHILE OTHERS HAVE NOT.

WHILE ALL OF GOD'S PROMISES ARE "YES" IN CHRIST, MANY OF THEM HAVE BEEN TRANSFORMED IN LIGHT OF THE GOSPEL.

ALL OF GOD'S PROMISES ARE FOR HIS GLORY AND OUR GOOD.

Since God's promises in the Bible were spoken into precise moments in history, some of them have already been fulfilled, while others are yet to be realized. In some instances, a promise can have more than one fulfillment.

The gospel is part of the "mystery of God" revealed in Jesus Christ (1Co 2:1). As such, it is bigger and better than anything we can imagine. Many of God's promises in the Old Testament find a deeper and broader fulfillment in the New Testament.

Redemptive history is leading us into a world "filled with the knowledge of the Lord's glory, as the water covers the sea" (Hab 2:14). At the same time, we know that God is working "all things…together for the good of those who love God, who are called according to his purpose" (Rm 8:28). Therefore, we can be confident that every promise in Scripture will lead toward these ends, though their ultimate fulfillment is likely to be beyond anything we can ask or imagine: "What no eye has seen, no ear has heard, and no human heart has conceived—God has prepared these things for those who love him" (1Co 2:9).

Generations after Abraham's death, when Joshua led the Israelites into Canaan to take possession of it, God's promise to give Abraham's descendants that land was fulfilled. However, their continued residence in the land was dependent on their obedience to the covenant He made with them through Moses (Jos 1:1–9).

In his letter to the Galatians, the apostle Paul wrote, "And if you belong to Christ, then you are Abraham's seed, heirs according to the promise" (Gl 3:29). Christ Himself is the blessing God promised the nations, and our claim as believers and heirs is not merely the land of Canaan. Rather, "the promise to Abraham" is "that he would inherit the world" (Rm 4:13).

"Abram believed the Lord, and he credited it to him as righteousness" (Gn 15:6). Abraham had faith, but at the time he could not have known that one of his descendants would be the Savior the world was waiting on. All of God's promises have been fulfilled in Christ, the author of everything good, beautiful, and true.

1

WEEK

OLD TESTAMENT PROMISES FULFILLED <u>IN</u> CHRIST

The Lord made promises to His people throughout the Old Testament. Some of these promises were made to individual people, like Abraham and David, while others were made to God's people as a whole. Some have already been fulfilled, and some will not reach the full extent of their fulfillment until the new heavens and the new earth. But all of these promises, as we will read in Day 1, are true in Christ (2Co 1:20).

THE PROMISES OF GOD ARE "YES" IN CHRIST

ESSAY

As we explore different promises found in the Old Testament, we begin with the New Testament assurance that "no matter how many promises God has made, they are "Yes" in Christ" (2Co 1:20 NIV). Jesus himself, God who came in the flesh, "is before all things," including the promises made in the Old Testament. It is through Him that all things hold together (Col 1:17).

Jesus Himself affirmed that the promises in the Old Testament find their fulfillment in Him, "beginning with Moses and all the prophets" (Lk 24:27). And as those living on the other side of Jesus's resurrection, we get to look at the whole of Scripture and see that we follow a "faithful God who keeps his gracious covenant loyalty for a thousand generations" (Dt 7:9). So as you read the Old Testament promises this week, join with us in saying "'Amen' to the glory of God" that they find their ultimate fulfillment in Christ (2Co 1:20).

2 CORINTHIANS 1:20 NIV

For no matter how many promises God has made, they are "Yes" in Christ. And so through him the "Amen" is spoken by us to the glory of God.

EXODUS 34:4-7

[4] Moses cut two stone tablets like the first ones. He got up early in the morning, and taking the two stone tablets in his hand, he climbed Mount Sinai, just as the LORD had commanded him.

[5] The LORD came down in a cloud, stood with him there, and proclaimed his name, "the LORD." [6] The LORD passed in front of him and proclaimed:

> The LORD—the LORD is a compassionate and gracious God, slow to anger and abounding in faithful love and truth, [7] maintaining faithful love to a thousand generations, forgiving iniquity, rebellion, and sin. But he will not leave the guilty unpunished, bringing the consequences of the fathers' iniquity on the children and grandchildren to the third and fourth generation.

DEUTERONOMY 7:9

Know that the LORD your God is God,

the faithful God who keeps his gracious covenant loyalty for a thousand generations

with those who love him and keep his commands.

LUKE 24:13-31

THE EMMAUS DISCIPLES

[13] Now that same day two of them were on their way to a village called Emmaus, which was about seven miles from Jerusalem. [14] Together they were discussing everything that had taken place. [15] And while they were discussing and arguing, Jesus himself came near and began to walk along with them. [16] But they were prevented from recognizing him. [17] Then he asked them, "What is this dispute that you're having with each other as you are walking?" And they stopped walking and looked discouraged.

18 The one named Cleopas answered him, "Are you the only visitor in Jerusalem who doesn't know the things that happened there in these days?"

19 "What things?" he asked them.

So they said to him, "The things concerning Jesus of Nazareth, who was a prophet powerful in action and speech before God and all the people, 20 and how our chief priests and leaders handed him over to be sentenced to death, and they crucified him. 21 But we were hoping that he was the one who was about to redeem Israel. Besides all this, it's the third day since these things happened. 22 Moreover, some women from our group astounded us. They arrived early at the tomb, 23 and when they didn't find his body, they came and reported that they had seen a vision of angels who said he was alive. 24 Some of those who were with us went to the tomb and found it just as the women had said, but they didn't see him."

25 He said to them, "How foolish you are, and how slow to believe all that the prophets have spoken! 26 Wasn't it necessary for the Messiah to suffer these things and enter into his glory?" 27 Then beginning with Moses and all the Prophets, he interpreted for them the things concerning himself in all the Scriptures.

28 They came near the village where they were going, and he gave the impression that he was going farther. 29 But they urged him, "Stay with us, because it's almost evening, and now the day is almost over." So he went in to stay with them.

30 It was as he reclined at the table with them that he took the bread, blessed and broke it, and gave it to them. 31 Then their eyes were opened, and they recognized him, but he disappeared from their sight.

COLOSSIANS 1:15–20

THE CENTRALITY OF CHRIST

15 He is the image of the invisible God,
the firstborn over all creation.
16 For everything was created by him,
in heaven and on earth,
the visible and the invisible,
whether thrones or dominions
or rulers or authorities—
all things have been created through him and
      for him.
17 He is before all things,
and by him all things hold together.
18 He is also the head of the body, the church;
he is the beginning,
the firstborn from the dead,
so that he might come to have
first place in everything.
19 For God was pleased to have
all his fullness dwell in him,
20 and through him to reconcile
everything to himself,
whether things on earth or things in heaven,
by making peace
through his blood, shed on the cross.

Use the prompts at the end of each reading day as a starting point for your own written prayer. Let each day's reading shape your prayer, thanking God for how His promises are being revealed to you specifically throughout each passage of Scripture. You can also use this space to ask the Lord for help in believing these promises.

THANK YOU THAT ALL OF YOUR PROMISES ARE "YES" THROUGH THE LIFE, DEATH, AND RESURRECTION OF CHRIST.

I WILL BLESS YOU

ESSAY

In Genesis 12, amid the chaos and brokenness in the opening narratives of Scripture, we find a command with a promise. God established a covenant with Abraham, promising to make him into a great nation. From Abraham, the blessing of that promise would extend to all the peoples of the earth. The Lord was establishing a covenant family, the people of God.

Galatians 3:16 says, "The promises were spoken to Abraham and to his seed," and that seed is Christ. Abraham had faith in the promise, and today we get to have faith in the One who fulfilled the promise. Through the New Testament authors, we see that the blessings of Abraham "will be credited to us who believe in him who raised Jesus our Lord from the dead" (Rm 4:24). Therefore, those who are in Christ have been grafted into this blessing that God first promised Abraham.

GENESIS 12:1-7

THE CALL OF ABRAM

¹ The Lord said to Abram:

> Go from your land,
> your relatives,
> and your father's house
> to the land that I will show you.
> ² I will make you into a great nation,
> I will bless you,
> I will make your name great,
> and you will be a blessing.
> ³ I will bless those who bless you,
> I will curse anyone who treats you with contempt,
> and all the peoples on earth
> will be blessed through you.

⁴ So Abram went, as the Lord had told him, and Lot went with him. Abram was seventy-five years old when he left Haran. ⁵ He took his wife, Sarai, his nephew Lot, all the possessions they had accumulated, and the people they had acquired in Haran, and they set out for the land of Canaan. When they came to the land of Canaan, ⁶ Abram passed through the land to the site of Shechem, at the oak of Moreh. (At that time the Canaanites were in the land.) ⁷ The Lord appeared to Abram and said, "To your offspring I will give this land." So he built an altar there to the Lord who had appeared to him.

GALATIANS 3:15-29

¹⁵ Brothers and sisters, I'm using a human illustration. No one sets aside or makes additions to a validated human will. ¹⁶ Now the promises were spoken to Abraham and to his seed. He does not say "and to seeds," as though referring to many, but referring to one, and to your seed, who is Christ. ¹⁷ My point is this: The law, which came 430 years later, does not invalidate a covenant previously established by God and thus cancel the promise. ¹⁸ For if the inheritance is based on the law, it is no longer based on the promise; but God has graciously given it to Abraham through the promise.

[19] Why, then, was the law given? It was added for the sake of transgressions until the Seed to whom the promise was made would come. The law was put into effect through angels by means of a mediator. [20] Now a mediator is not just for one person alone, but God is one. [21] Is the law therefore contrary to God's promises? Absolutely not! For if the law had been granted with the ability to give life, then righteousness would certainly be on the basis of the law. [22] But the Scripture imprisoned everything under sin's power, so that the promise might be given on the basis of faith in Jesus Christ to those who believe. [23] Before this faith came, we were confined under the law, imprisoned until the coming faith was revealed. [24] The law, then, was our guardian until Christ, so that we could be justified by faith. [25] But since that faith has come, we are no longer under a guardian, [26] for through faith you are all sons of God in Christ Jesus.

SONS AND HEIRS

[27] For those of you who were baptized into Christ have been clothed with Christ. [28] There is no Jew or Greek, slave or free, male and female; since you are all one in Christ Jesus. [29] And if you belong to Christ, then you are Abraham's seed, heirs according to the promise.

ROMANS 4:13-25

THE PROMISE GRANTED THROUGH FAITH

[13] For the promise to Abraham or to his descendants that he would inherit the world was not through the law, but through the righteousness that comes by faith. [14] If those who are of the law are heirs, faith is made empty and the promise nullified, [15] because the law produces wrath. And where there is no law, there is no transgression.

[16] This is why the promise is by faith, so that it may be according to grace, to guarantee it to all the descendants—

not only to the one who is of the law but also to the one who is of Abraham's faith. He is the father of us all. [17] As it is written: I have made you the father of many nations—in the presence of the God in whom he believed, the one who gives life to the dead and calls things into existence that do not exist. [18] He believed, hoping against hope, so that he became the father of many nations according to what had been spoken: So will your descendants be. [19] He did not weaken in faith when he considered his own body to be already dead (since he was about a hundred years old) and also the deadness of Sarah's womb. [20] He did not waver in unbelief at God's promise but was strengthened in his faith and gave glory to God, [21] because he was fully convinced that what God had promised, he was also able to do. [22] Therefore, it was credited to him for righteousness. [23] Now it was credited to him was not written for Abraham alone, [24] but also for us. It will be credited to us who believe in him who raised Jesus our Lord from the dead. [25] He was delivered up for our trespasses and raised for our justification.

HEBREWS 11:8–16

[8] By faith Abraham, when he was called, obeyed and set out for a place that he was going to receive as an inheritance. He went out, even though he did not know where he was going. [9] By faith he stayed as a foreigner in the land of promise, living in tents as did Isaac and Jacob, coheirs of the same promise. [10] For he was looking forward to the city that has foundations, whose architect and builder is God.

[11] By faith even Sarah herself, when she was unable to have children, received power to conceive offspring, even though she was past the age, since she considered that the one who had promised was faithful. [12] Therefore, from one man—in fact, from one as good as dead—came offspring as numerous as the stars of the sky and as innumerable as the grains of sand along the seashore.

[13] These all died in faith, although they had not received the things that were promised. But they saw them from a distance, greeted them, and confessed that they were foreigners and temporary residents on the earth. [14] Now those who say such things make it clear that they are seeking a homeland. [15] If they were thinking about where they came from, they would have had an opportunity to return. [16] But they now desire a better place—a heavenly one. Therefore, God is not ashamed to be called their God, for he has prepared a city for them.

THANK YOU FOR YOUR
PROMISE THAT BEGAN WITH
ABRAHAM AND THE BLESSING
THAT HAS BEEN EXTENDED
TO ME IN CHRIST.

SAYINGS AND SCRIPTURE

Wisdom can come from many places, but only God's Word offers enduring promises anchored in unshakable truth. Listed here are common sayings that sound like promises from Scripture but originated from another source or oversimplify a verse's original intent. Along with the sayings, you'll find an explanation of the biblical context and relevant Scripture.

GOD WON'T GIVE YOU MORE THAN YOU CAN HANDLE.

God never promises that we'll be able to handle all the difficulties that come our way. Instead, He promises to provide a way of escape for temptations of every kind and to give us His strength when we need it.

No temptation has come upon you except what is common to humanity. But God is faithful; he will not allow you to be tempted beyond what you are able, but with the temptation he will also provide a way out so that you may be able to bear it.

1CO 10:13

But he said to me, "My grace is sufficient for you, for my power is perfected in weakness." Therefore, I will most gladly boast all the more about my weaknesses, so that Christ's power may reside in me.

2CO 12:9

WHEN GOD CLOSES A DOOR, HE OPENS A WINDOW.

When an opportunity doesn't go the way we'd hoped, God doesn't necessarily bring about a better one. But He does promise to comfort us.

"Blessed are those who mourn, for they will be comforted."

MT 5:4

EVERYTHING HAPPENS FOR A REASON.

We don't always know why God allows certain things in our lives, but He does promise that He is holding all things together and that He is in control.

Oh, the depth of the riches
and the wisdom and the
    knowledge of God!
How unsearchable
    his judgments
and untraceable his ways!
For who has known the
    mind of the Lord?
Or who has been
    his counselor?
And who has ever given
    to God,
that he should be repaid?
For from him and
    through him
and to him are all things.
To him be the glory
    forever. Amen.

RM 11:33–36

THIS TOO SHALL PASS.

This is an oversimplification of a beautiful promise. While we will have pain in this life and may struggle to navigate that pain, Jesus is with us as we suffer and is preparing an eternal home for us.

For our momentary light
affliction is producing
for us an absolutely
incomparable eternal
weight of glory. So we do
not focus on what is seen,
but on what is unseen.
For what is seen is
temporary, but what is
unseen is eternal.

2CO 4:17–18

GOD HELPS THOSE WHO HELP THEMSELVES.

While we may value personal ingenuity, wise stewardship, and hard work, we also acknowledge that we are ultimately dependent on God for His provision and care.

"But seek his kingdom, and
these things will be provided
for you. Don't be afraid,
little flock, because your
Father delights to give you
the kingdom."

LK 12:31–32

CLEANLINESS IS NEXT TO GODLINESS.

This phrase is recorded in a sermon by John Wesley, but it may stem from an ancient Babylonian or Hebrew concept. Although we can't earn salvation or merit through external acts, Scripture often depicts physical cleansing as a sign of spiritual cleansing or restoration.

Jesus replied, "If I don't
wash you, you have no part
with me."

Simon Peter said to him,
"Lord, not only my feet, but
also my hands and my head."

"One who has bathed,"
Jesus told him, "doesn't
need to wash anything
except his feet, but he is
completely clean…"

JN 13:8–10

GOOD THINGS COME TO THOSE WHO WAIT.

While there isn't a cause-and-effect relationship between the act of waiting and material good fortune, we do know that our actions have eternal consequences.

Let us not get tired of
doing good, for we will
reap at the proper time
if we don't give up.

GL 6:9

I WILL NOT LEAVE
YOU <u>OR</u> ABANDON YOU

ESSAY

Throughout the Old Testament, the Lord revealed His plans to His people and how they were to take hold of His promises. After Moses's death, Joshua was charged with leading God's people into the land God promised to them. And as they traveled, they carried a very tangible reminder of God's presence with them: the ark of the covenant.

Those who went forward with Joshua walked with the presence of God guiding and protecting them. And because of Jesus's resurrection, we now can live in the reality of what Jesus told His own disciples, "I am in my Father, you are in me, and I am in you" (Jn 14:20). The promise of life in God's eternal presence is extended to all those who follow and obey Jesus. His presence is the good promise we have been given, wherever we may go (Ps 73:28).

JOSHUA 1:1-9

ENCOURAGEMENT OF JOSHUA

[1] After the death of Moses the LORD's servant, the LORD spoke to Joshua son of Nun, Moses's assistant: [2] "Moses my servant is dead. Now you and all the people prepare to cross over the Jordan to the land I am giving the Israelites. [3] I have given you every place where the sole of your foot treads, just as I promised Moses. [4] Your territory will be from the wilderness and Lebanon to the great river, the Euphrates River—all the land of the Hittites—and west to the Mediterranean Sea. [5] No one will be able to stand against you as long as you live. I will be with you, just as I was with Moses. I will not leave you or abandon you.

[6] "Be strong and courageous, for you will distribute the land I swore to their ancestors to give them as an inheritance. [7] Above all, be strong and very courageous to observe carefully the whole instruction my servant Moses commanded you. Do not turn from it to the right or the left, so that you will have success wherever you go. [8] This book of instruction must not depart from your mouth; you are to meditate on it day and night so that you may carefully observe everything written in it. For then you will prosper and succeed in whatever you do. [9] Haven't I commanded you: be strong and courageous? Do not be afraid or discouraged, for the LORD your God is with you wherever you go."

JOSHUA 3:1-17

CROSSING THE JORDAN

[1] Joshua started early the next morning and left the Acacia Grove with all the Israelites. They went as far as the Jordan and stayed there before crossing. [2] After three days the officers went through the camp [3] and commanded the people, "When you see the ark of the covenant of the LORD your God carried by the Levitical priests, you are to break camp and follow it. [4] But keep a distance of about a thousand yards between yourselves and the ark. Don't go near it, so that you can see the way to go, for you haven't traveled this way before."

[5] Joshua told the people, "Consecrate yourselves, because the LORD will do wonders among you tomorrow." [6] Then he said to the priests, "Carry the ark of the covenant and go on ahead of the people." So they carried the ark of the covenant and went ahead of them.

⁷ The LORD spoke to Joshua:

"Today I will begin to exalt you in the sight of all Israel, so they will know that I will be with you just as I was with Moses.

⁸ Command the priests carrying the ark of the covenant: When you reach the edge of the water, stand in the Jordan."

⁹ Then Joshua told the Israelites, "Come closer and listen to the words of the LORD your God." ¹⁰ He said, "You will know that the living God is among you and that he will certainly dispossess before you the Canaanites, Hethites, Hivites, Perizzites, Girgashites, Amorites, and Jebusites ¹¹ when the ark of the covenant of the Lord of the whole earth goes ahead of you into the Jordan. ¹² Now choose twelve men from the tribes of Israel, one man for each tribe. ¹³ When the feet of the priests who carry the ark of the LORD, the Lord of the whole earth, come to rest in the Jordan's water, its water will be cut off. The water flowing downstream will stand up in a mass."

¹⁴ When the people broke camp to cross the Jordan, the priests carried the ark of the covenant ahead of the people. ¹⁵ Now the Jordan overflows its banks throughout the harvest season. But as soon as the priests carrying the ark reached the Jordan, their feet touched the water at its edge ¹⁶ and the water flowing downstream stood still, rising up in a mass that extended as far as Adam, a city next to Zarethan. The water flowing downstream into the Sea of the Arabah—the Dead Sea—was completely cut off, and the people crossed opposite Jericho. ¹⁷ The priests carrying the ark of the LORD's covenant stood firmly on dry ground in the middle of the Jordan, while all Israel crossed on dry ground until the entire nation had finished crossing the Jordan.

PSALM 73:21–28

²¹ When I became embittered
and my innermost being was wounded,
²² I was stupid and didn't understand;
I was an unthinking animal toward you.
²³ Yet I am always with you;
you hold my right hand.
²⁴ You guide me with your counsel,
and afterward you will take me up in glory.

²⁵ Who do I have in heaven but you?
And I desire nothing on earth but you.
²⁶ My flesh and my heart may fail,
but God is the strength of my heart,
my portion forever.
²⁷ Those far from you will certainly perish;
you destroy all who are unfaithful to you.
²⁸ But as for me, God's presence is my good.
I have made the Lord GOD my refuge,
so I can tell about all you do.

JOHN 14:18-24

THE FATHER, THE SON, AND THE HOLY SPIRIT

¹⁸ "I will not leave you as orphans; I am coming to you. ¹⁹ In a little while the world will no longer see me, but you will see me. Because I live, you will live too. ²⁰ On that day you will know that I am in my Father, you are in me, and I am in you. ²¹ The one who has my commands and keeps them is the one who loves me. And the one who loves me will be loved by my Father. I also will love him and will reveal myself to him."

²² Judas (not Iscariot) said to him, "Lord, how is it you're going to reveal yourself to us and not to the world?"

²³ Jesus answered, "If anyone loves me, he will keep my word. My Father will love him, and we will come to him and make our home with him. ²⁴ The one who doesn't love me will not keep my words. The word that you hear is not mine but is from the Father who sent me."

THANK YOU FOR YOUR
PROMISE TO NEVER LEAVE
OR ABANDON YOUR PEOPLE,
INCLUDING ME.

I WILL GIVE YOU ᴀɴ EVERLASTING KINGDOM

ESSAY

The Lord made a promise to King David, in the newly established kingdom of Israel that his house and kingdom would endure forever (2Sm 7:16). David lived and died, and many kings followed. Yet still, David was a finite man who received an eternal promise.

Jesus is the eternal King who sits on David's throne. But more than that, He sits at the right hand of the Father. His kingdom is spread across the whole earth as the gospel is preached and received, until one day when it will be said, "The kingdom of the world has become the kingdom of our Lord and of his Christ" (Rv 11:15). In Christ, we are now citizens of His kingdom, and when He returns, we will reign with Him.

2 SAMUEL 7:4–17

[4] But that night the word of the LORD came to Nathan: [5] "Go to my servant David and say, 'This is what the LORD says: Are you to build me a house to dwell in? [6] From the time I brought the Israelites out of Egypt until today I have not dwelt in a house; instead, I have been moving around with a tent as my dwelling. [7] In all my journeys with all the Israelites, have I ever spoken a word to one of the tribal leaders of Israel, whom I commanded to shepherd my people Israel, asking: Why haven't you built me a house of cedar?'

[8] "So now this is what you are to say to my servant David: 'This is what the LORD of Armies says: I took you from the pasture, from tending the flock, to be ruler over my people Israel. [9] I have been with you wherever you have gone, and I have destroyed all your enemies before you. I will make a great name for you like that of the greatest on the earth. [10] I will designate a place for my people Israel and plant them, so that they may live there and not be disturbed again. Evildoers will not continue to oppress them as they have done [11] ever since the day I ordered judges to be over my people Israel. I will give you rest from all your enemies.

"'The LORD declares to you: The LORD himself will make a house for you. [12] When your time comes and you rest with your ancestors, I will raise up after you your descendant, who will come from your body, and I will establish his kingdom. [13] He is the one who will build a house for my name, and I will establish the throne of his kingdom forever. [14] I will be his father, and he will be my son. When he does wrong, I will discipline him with a rod of men and blows from mortals. [15] But my faithful love will never leave him as it did when I removed it from Saul, whom I removed from before you. [16] Your house and kingdom will endure before me forever, and your throne will be established forever.'"

[17] Nathan reported all these words and this entire vision to David.

2 The people walking in darkness
have seen a great light;
a light has dawned
on those living in the land of darkness.
3 You have enlarged the nation
and increased its joy.
The people have rejoiced before you
as they rejoice at harvest time
and as they rejoice when dividing spoils.
4 For you have shattered their oppressive yoke
and the rod on their shoulders,
the staff of their oppressor,
just as you did on the day of Midian.
5 For every trampling boot of battle
and the bloodied garments of war
will be burned as fuel for the fire.
6 For a child will be born for us,
a son will be given to us,
and the government will be on his shoulders.
He will be named
Wonderful Counselor, Mighty God,
Eternal Father, Prince of Peace.

7 The dominion will be vast,
and its prosperity will never end.
He will reign on the throne of David
and over his kingdom,
to establish and sustain it
with justice and righteousness from now
    on and forever.

The zeal of the Lord of Armies will accomplish this.

ISAIAH 11:1-9

REIGN OF THE DAVIDIC KING

[1] Then a shoot will grow from the stump of Jesse,
and a branch from his roots will bear fruit.
[2] The Spirit of the Lord will rest on him—
a Spirit of wisdom and understanding,
a Spirit of counsel and strength,
a Spirit of knowledge and of the fear of the Lord.
[3] His delight will be in the fear of the Lord.
He will not judge
by what he sees with his eyes,
he will not execute justice
by what he hears with his ears,
[4] but he will judge the poor righteously
and execute justice for the oppressed of the land.
He will strike the land
with a scepter from his mouth,
and he will kill the wicked
with a command from his lips.
[5] Righteousness will be a belt around his hips;
faithfulness will be a belt around his waist.

[6] The wolf will dwell with the lamb,
and the leopard will lie down with the goat.
The calf, the young lion, and the fattened calf will be together,
and a child will lead them.
[7] The cow and the bear will graze,
their young ones will lie down together,
and the lion will eat straw like cattle.
[8] An infant will play beside the cobra's pit,
and a toddler will put his hand into a snake's den.
[9] They will not harm or destroy each other
on my entire holy mountain,
for the land will be as full
of the knowledge of the Lord
as the sea is filled with water.

He was given dominion
and glory and a kingdom,
so that those of every people,
nation, and language
should serve him.
His dominion is an everlasting dominion
that will not pass away,
and his kingdom is one
that will not be destroyed.

MATTHEW 4:12–17

MINISTRY IN GALILEE

[12] When he heard that John had been arrested, he withdrew into Galilee.
[13] He left Nazareth and went to live in Capernaum by the sea, in the
region of Zebulun and Naphtali. [14] This was to fulfill what was spoken
through the prophet Isaiah:

[15] Land of Zebulun and land of Naphtali,
along the road by the sea, beyond the Jordan,
Galilee of the Gentiles.
[16] The people who live in darkness
have seen a great light,
and for those living in the land of the shadow of death,
a light has dawned.

[17] From then on Jesus began to preach, "Repent, because the kingdom of
heaven has come near."

REVELATION 11:15–17

THE SEVENTH TRUMPET

[15] The seventh angel blew his trumpet, and there were loud voices in
heaven saying,

> The kingdom of the world has become the kingdom
> of our Lord and of his Christ,
> and he will reign forever and ever.

[16] The twenty-four elders, who were seated before God on their thrones, fell facedown and worshiped God, [17] saying,

> We give you thanks, Lord God, the Almighty,
> who is and who was,
> because you have taken your great power
> and have begun to reign.

2 TIMOTHY 2:8-13

[8] Remember Jesus Christ, risen from the dead and descended from David, according to my gospel, [9] for which I suffer to the point of being bound like a criminal. But the word of God is not bound. [10] This is why I endure all things for the elect: so that they also may obtain salvation, which is in Christ Jesus, with eternal glory. [11] This saying is trustworthy:

> For if we died with him,
> we will also live with him;
> [12] if we endure, we will also reign with him;
> if we deny him, he will also deny us;
> [13] if we are faithless, he remains faithful,
> for he cannot deny himself.

THANK YOU FOR YOUR
PROMISE TO REIGN FOREVER
AS KING OVER ALL.

I WILL GIVE YOU A
FUTURE <u>AND</u> A HOPE

ESSAY

This promise of purposeful plans is found within a letter sent by the prophet Jeremiah to the people of Judah after they had been taken into captivity by the nation of Babylon. This captivity, also known as the exile, was an expression of God's judgment against the nation of Judah for their unfaithfulness to Him. Received early on in the exile, this letter encouraged the people of Judah to make their home in Babylon (Jr 29:4–7). But this challenging command was accompanied by the assurance of God's purposeful plans for His people. These were plans for their "well-being, not for disaster, to give…a future and a hope" (Jr 29:11), which included their restoration as a nation and their return from Babylon back to the promised land.

These promises were for the same nation through which the promised Savior would come. The good plans we get to trust in today are found in the redemptive plan of Jesus for us and our sin. We who had been exiled from the presence of God because of sin now have a future and a hope because of Christ's life, death, and resurrection.

JEREMIAH 29:1–14

JEREMIAH'S LETTER TO THE EXILES

[1] This is the text of the letter that the prophet Jeremiah sent from Jerusalem to the remaining exiled elders, the priests, the prophets, and all the people Nebuchadnezzar had deported from Jerusalem to Babylon. [2] This was after King Jeconiah, the queen mother, the court officials, the officials of Judah and Jerusalem, the craftsmen, and the metalsmiths had left Jerusalem. [3] He sent the letter with Elasah son of Shaphan and Gemariah son of Hilkiah, whom Zedekiah king of Judah sent to Babylon to King Nebuchadnezzar of Babylon. The letter stated:

[4] This is what the LORD of Armies, the God of Israel, says to all the exiles I deported from Jerusalem to Babylon: [5] "Build houses and live in them. Plant gardens and eat their produce. [6] Find wives for yourselves, and have sons and daughters. Find wives for your sons and give your daughters to men in marriage so that they may bear sons and daughters. Multiply there; do not decrease. [7] Pursue the well-being of the city I have deported you to. Pray to the LORD on its behalf, for when it thrives, you will thrive."

[8] For this is what the LORD of Armies, the God of Israel, says: "Don't let your prophets who are among you and your diviners deceive you, and don't listen to the dreams you elicit from them, [9] for they are prophesying falsely to you in my name. I have not sent them." This is the LORD's declaration.

[10] For this is what the LORD says: "When seventy years for Babylon are complete, I will attend to you and will confirm my promise concerning you to restore you to this place. [11] For I know the plans I have for you"—this is the LORD's declaration—"plans for your well-being, not for disaster, to give you a future and a hope. [12] You will call to me and come and pray to me, and I will listen to you. [13] You will seek me and find me when you search for me with all your heart. [14] I will be found by you"—this is the LORD's declaration—"and I will restore your fortunes and gather you from all the nations and places where I banished you"—this is the LORD's declaration. "I will restore you to the place from which I deported you."

SACRIFICE RESTORED

¹ When the seventh month arrived, and the Israelites were in their towns, the people gathered as one in Jerusalem. ² Jeshua son of Jozadak and his brothers the priests along with Zerubbabel son of Shealtiel and his brothers began to build the altar of Israel's God in order to offer burnt offerings on it, as it is written in the law of Moses, the man of God. ³ They set up the altar on its foundation and offered burnt offerings for the morning and evening on it to the LORD even though they feared the surrounding peoples. ⁴ They celebrated the Festival of Shelters as prescribed, and offered burnt offerings each day, based on the number specified by ordinance for each festival day. ⁵ After that, they offered the regular burnt offering and the offerings for the beginning of each month and for all the LORD's appointed holy occasions, as well as the freewill offerings brought to the LORD.

⁶ On the first day of the seventh month they began to offer burnt offerings to the LORD, even though the foundation of the LORD's temple had not yet been laid. ⁷ They gave money to the stonecutters and artisans, and gave food, drink, and oil to the people of Sidon and Tyre, so they would bring cedar wood from Lebanon to Joppa by sea, according to the authorization given them by King Cyrus of Persia.

REBUILDING THE TEMPLE

⁸ In the second month of the second year after they arrived at God's house in Jerusalem, Zerubbabel son of Shealtiel, Jeshua son of Jozadak, and the rest of their brothers, including the priests, the Levites, and all who had returned to Jerusalem from the captivity, began to build. They appointed the Levites who were twenty years old or more to supervise the work on the LORD's house. ⁹ Jeshua with his sons and brothers, Kadmiel with his sons, and the sons of Judah and of Henadad, with their sons and brothers, the Levites, joined together to supervise those working on the house of God.

TEMPLE FOUNDATION COMPLETED

¹⁰ When the builders had laid the foundation of the LORD's temple, the priests, dressed in their robes and holding trumpets, and the Levites descended from Asaph, holding cymbals, took their positions to praise

the LORD, as King David of Israel had instructed. [11] They sang with praise and thanksgiving to the LORD: "For he is good; his faithful love to Israel endures forever." Then all the people gave a great shout of praise to the LORD because the foundation of the LORD's house had been laid.

2 CORINTHIANS 4:7–15

TREASURE IN CLAY JARS

[7] Now we have this treasure in clay jars, so that this extraordinary power may be from God and not from us. [8] We are afflicted in every way but not crushed; we are perplexed but not in despair; [9] we are persecuted but not abandoned; we are struck down but not destroyed. [10] We always carry the death of Jesus in our body, so that the life of Jesus may also be displayed in our body. [11] For we who live are always being given over to death for Jesus's sake, so that Jesus's life may also be displayed in our mortal flesh. [12] So then, death is at work in us, but life in you. [13] And since we have the same spirit of faith in keeping with what is written, I believed, therefore I spoke, we also believe, and therefore speak. [14] For we know that the one who raised the Lord Jesus will also raise us with Jesus and present us with you. [15] Indeed, everything is for your benefit so that, as grace extends through more and more people, it may cause thanksgiving to increase to the glory of God.

EPHESIANS 1:11–14

[11] In him we have also received an inheritance, because we were predestined according to the plan of the one who works out everything in agreement with the purpose of his will,

[12] so that we who had already put our hope in Christ might bring praise to his glory.

[13] In him you also were sealed with the promised Holy Spirit when you heard the word of truth, the gospel of your salvation, and when you believed. [14] The Holy Spirit is the down payment of our inheritance, until the redemption of the possession, to the praise of his glory.

THANK YOU FOR YOUR
PROMISE TO KEEP MY FUTURE
AND HOPE ETERNALLY SECURE
IN CHRIST.

GRACE DAY

Take this day to catch up on your reading,
pray, and rest in the presence of the Lord.

KNOW THAT GOD IS GOD, GOD WHO KEEPS COVENANT THOUSAND WITH THOSE WHO KEEP HIS

THE LORD YOUR THE FAITHFUL HIS GRACIOUS LOYALTY FOR A GENERATIONS LOVE HIM AND COMMANDS.

DEUTERONOMY 7:9

WEEKLY

LY

TR

UTH

07

DAY

Scripture is God breathed and true. When we memorize it,
we carry the good news of Jesus with us wherever we go.

Throughout this reading plan, we will memorize our key
verse for this plan. This week we will start with the first half.

FOR NO MATTER HOW MANY PROMISES GOD HAS MADE, THEY ARE "YES" IN CHRIST. AND SO THROUGH HIM THE "AMEN" IS SPOKEN BY US TO THE GLORY OF GOD.

---

2 CORINTHIANS 1:20 NIV

See tips for memorizing Scripture on page 124.

2

WEEK

CHRIST'S PROMISES <u>TO</u> ALL BELIEVERS

In the New Testament, Jesus made promises to His followers that are also true for believers today. These promises are rooted in the gospel story—the truth that Christ's death and resurrection have saved us from our sins, are making us like Him, and have equipped us to share His love with others. Some of the promises Christ makes seem daunting at first, like His promise that all believers will endure persecution (Jn 16:33). However, alongside this promise of hardship are promises of peace, presence, and victory.

I WILL FORGIVE YOUR SINS

ESSAY

Luke records one last interaction between Jesus and His friends before He ascended into heaven. In it, we find a direct statement about one of His purposes as the Messiah: "The Messiah will suffer and rise from the dead the third day, and repentance for forgiveness of sins will be proclaimed in his name to all the nations" (Luke 24:46–47).

Thankfully, in this conversation Jesus didn't make any caveats, footnotes, or fine print about the kinds of sin covered by His sacrifice. No matter how dark or scandalous our personal sins may be, God extends forgiveness. As our perfect and sinless high priest, Jesus does not have need for someone to forgive His sin and is able to cover the sin of all who believe in Him. Once we take hold of this promise and feel the weight of our sin removed because of Christ, we are charged to share that freedom and hope with the world.

MATTHEW 26:26–28

THE FIRST LORD'S SUPPER

[26] As they were eating, Jesus took bread, blessed and broke it, gave it to the disciples, and said, "Take and eat it; this is my body." [27] Then he took a cup, and after giving thanks, he gave it to them and said, "Drink from it, all of you. [28] For this is my blood of the covenant, which is poured out for many for the forgiveness of sins.

COLOSSIANS 1:13–14

[13] He has rescued us from the domain of darkness and transferred us into the kingdom of the Son he loves. [14] In him we have redemption, the forgiveness of sins.

HEBREWS 7:26–28

[26] For this is the kind of high priest we need: holy, innocent, undefiled, separated from sinners, and exalted above the heavens.

[27] He doesn't need to offer sacrifices every day, as high priests do—first for their own sins, then for those of the people.

He did this once for all time when he offered himself. [28] For the law appoints as high priests men who are weak, but the promise of the oath, which came after the law, appoints a Son, who has been perfected forever.

HEBREWS 8:7–13

[7] For if that first covenant had been faultless, there would have been no occasion for a second one. [8] But finding fault with his people, he says:

See, the days are coming, says the Lord,
when I will make a new covenant
with the house of Israel
and with the house of Judah—
[9] not like the covenant
that I made with their ancestors

on the day I took them by the hand
to lead them out of the land of Egypt.
I showed no concern for them, says the Lord,
because they did not continue in my covenant.
[10] For this is the covenant
that I will make with the house of Israel
after those days, says the Lord:
I will put my laws into their minds
and write them on their hearts.
I will be their God,
and they will be my people.
[11] And each person will not teach his fellow citizen,
and each his brother or sister, saying, "Know the Lord,"
because they will all know me,
from the least to the greatest of them.
[12] For I will forgive their wrongdoing,
and I will never again remember their sins.

[13] By saying a new covenant, he has declared that the first is obsolete. And what is obsolete and growing old is about to pass away.

EPHESIANS 1:7-8

[7] In him we have redemption through his blood, the forgiveness of our trespasses, according to the riches of his grace [8] that he richly poured out on us with all wisdom and understanding.

1 JOHN 1:5-10

[5] This is the message we have heard from him and declare to you: God is light, and there is absolutely no darkness in him. [6] If we say, "We have fellowship with him," and yet we walk in darkness, we are lying and are not practicing the truth. [7] If we walk in the light as he himself is in the light, we have fellowship with one another, and the blood of Jesus his Son cleanses us from all sin. [8] If we say, "We have no sin," we are deceiving ourselves, and the truth is not in us. [9] If we confess our sins, he is faithful and righteous to forgive us our sins and to cleanse us from all unrighteousness. [10] If we say, "We have not sinned," we make him a liar, and his word is not in us.

2 CORINTHIANS 5:18–19

[18] Everything is from God, who has reconciled us to himself through Christ and has given us the ministry of reconciliation. [19] That is, in Christ, God was reconciling the world to himself, not counting their trespasses against them, and he has committed the message of reconciliation to us.

Remember to use these prompts as a starting point for your prayer, letting each day's reading shape how you respond to God's promise. Thank Him for how His promises are revealed through Scripture, and ask the Lord for any ways you need help believing these promises.

THANK YOU FOR YOUR PROMISE TO FORGIVE MY SIN.

I WILL GIVE YOU PEACE AND REST

ESSAY

When you think of rest, you may envision a quiet weekend in a quaint cabin in the woods or perhaps a peaceful morning on the beach. The kind of rest Jesus offers isn't always a retreat but more of a new way of living drawn from the Old Testament concept of *shalom*. Shalom is more than rest; it is peace, wholeness, and connection to the Lord.

This is only possible when we learn to rely on God rather than our own efforts, to cast our worries onto His back rather than piling them up on our own. Jesus tells His followers that His "yoke is easy and [His] burden is light" (Mt 11:30). Jesus taught the way of the kingdom, complete with the pace and priorities of heaven, and He modeled total dependence on God, the key to true shalom. And while we may not always feel good about our circumstance or lead a trouble-free life, Jesus promises His peace as we rely on Him for strength, hope, and joy.

MATTHEW 11:28–30

[28] "Come to me, all of you who are weary and burdened, and I will give you rest. [29] Take up my yoke and learn from me, because I am lowly and humble in heart, and you will find rest for your souls. [30] For my yoke is easy and my burden is light."

JOHN 14:27

"Peace I leave with you. My peace I give to you. I do not give to you as the world gives. Don't let your heart be troubled or fearful."

JOHN 20:19–23

THE DISCIPLES COMMISSIONED

[19] When it was evening on that first day of the week, the disciples were gathered together with the doors locked because they feared the Jews. Jesus came, stood among them, and said to them, "Peace be with you."

[20] Having said this, he showed them his hands and his side. So the disciples rejoiced when they saw the Lord.

[21] Jesus said to them again, "Peace be with you. As the Father has sent me, I also send you." [22] After saying this, he breathed on them and said, "Receive the Holy Spirit. [23] If you forgive the sins of any, they are forgiven them; if you retain the sins of any, they are retained."

PSALM 55:22

Cast your burden on the LORD,
and he will sustain you;
he will never allow the righteous to be shaken.

ISAIAH 53:1–5

[1] Who has believed what we have heard?
And to whom has the arm of the LORD been revealed?
[2] He grew up before him like a young plant

and like a root out of dry ground.
He didn't have an impressive form
or majesty that we should look at him,
no appearance that we should desire him.
[3] He was despised and rejected by men,
a man of suffering who knew what
     sickness was.
He was like someone people turned
     away from;
he was despised, and we didn't value him.

[4] Yet he himself bore our sicknesses,
and he carried our pains;
but we in turn regarded him stricken,
struck down by God, and afflicted.
[5] But he was pierced because of our rebellion,
crushed because of our iniquities;
punishment for our peace was on him,
and we are healed by his wounds.

PHILIPPIANS 4:4-7

[4] Rejoice in the Lord always. I will say it again: Rejoice! [5] Let your graciousness be known to everyone. The Lord is near. [6] Don't worry about anything, but in everything, through prayer and petition with thanksgiving, present your requests to God. [7] And the peace of God, which surpasses all understanding, will guard your hearts and minds in Christ Jesus.

COLOSSIANS 3:12-17

THE CHRISTIAN LIFE

[12] Therefore, as God's chosen ones, holy and dearly loved, put on compassion, kindness, humility, gentleness, and patience, [13] bearing with one another and forgiving one another if anyone has a grievance against another. Just as the Lord has forgiven you, so you are also to forgive. [14] Above all, put on love, which is the perfect bond of unity. [15] And let the peace of Christ, to which you were also called in one body, rule your hearts. And be thankful. [16] Let the word of Christ dwell richly among you, in all wisdom teaching and admonishing one another through psalms, hymns, and spiritual songs, singing to God with gratitude in your hearts. [17] And whatever you do, in word or in deed, do everything in the name of the Lord Jesus, giving thanks to God the Father through him.

THANK YOU FOR YOUR
PROMISE OF PEACE THAT
CAN BE FOUND WHEN I AM
AT REST IN YOU.

I WILL GIVE YOU ABUNDANT LIFE

ESSAY

Jesus promised His followers everlasting life (more on that on Day 18), but the hope of the Christian life is so much more than that. He also spoke of a new life that starts right here and now, what John 10:10 describes as abundant life. It is abundant because it is the kind of life only God can provide—characterized by full freedom for the oppressed, healing for the brokenhearted, and joy for all who trust in Him (Is 61:1, 7).

How do we experience this abundant life? By abiding in Christ and allowing Him to grow in us the fruit of His Spirit (Jn 15:5), by drawing near and allowing Him to cleanse us of sin (Heb 10:22), and by living out Christ's love and goodness in our actions and encouragements with each other (Heb 10:23).

JOHN 10:7-10

[7] Jesus said again, "Truly I tell you, I am the gate for the sheep. [8] All who came before me are thieves and robbers, but the sheep didn't listen to them. [9] I am the gate. If anyone enters by me, he will be saved and will come in and go out and find pasture. [10] A thief comes only to steal and kill and destroy. I have come so that they may have life and have it in abundance."

ISAIAH 61:1-7

MESSIAH'S JUBILEE

[1] The Spirit of the Lord God is on me,
because the Lord has anointed me
to bring good news to the poor.

He has sent me to heal the brokenhearted,
to proclaim liberty to the captives
and freedom to the prisoners;

[2] to proclaim the year of the Lord's favor,
and the day of our God's vengeance;
to comfort all who mourn,
[3] to provide for those who mourn in Zion;
to give them a crown of beauty instead of ashes,
festive oil instead of mourning,
and splendid clothes instead of despair.
And they will be called righteous trees,
planted by the Lord
to glorify him.
[4] They will rebuild the ancient ruins;
they will restore the former devastations;
they will renew the ruined cities,
the devastations of many generations.
[5] Strangers will stand and feed your flocks,
and foreigners will be your plowmen and vinedressers.

⁶ But you will be called the LORD's priests;

they will speak of you as ministers of our God;

you will eat the wealth of the nations,

and you will boast in their riches.

⁷ In place of your shame, you will have a

    double portion;

in place of disgrace, they will rejoice over

    their share.

So they will possess double in their land,

and eternal joy will be theirs.

JOHN 15:1–11

THE VINE AND THE BRANCHES

¹ "I am the true vine, and my Father is the gardener. ² Every branch in me that does not produce fruit he removes, and he prunes every branch that produces fruit so that it will produce more fruit. ³ You are already clean because of the word I have spoken to you. ⁴ Remain in me, and I in you. Just as a branch is unable to produce fruit by itself unless it remains on the vine, neither can you unless you remain in me. ⁵ I am the vine; you are the branches. The one who remains in me and I in him produces much fruit, because you can do nothing without me. ⁶ If anyone does not remain in me, he is thrown aside like a branch and he withers. They gather them, throw them into the fire, and they are burned. ⁷ If you remain in me and my words remain in you, ask whatever you want and it will be done for you. ⁸ My Father is glorified by this: that you produce much fruit and prove to be my disciples.

CHRISTLIKE LOVE

⁹ "As the Father has loved me, I have also loved you. Remain in my love. ¹⁰ If you keep my commands you will remain in my love, just as I have kept my Father's commands and remain in his love.

¹¹ "I have told you these things so that my joy may be in you and your joy may be complete."

HEBREWS 10:19-25

EXHORTATIONS TO GODLINESS

[19] Therefore, brothers and sisters, since we have boldness to enter the sanctuary through the blood of Jesus— [20] he has inaugurated for us a new and living way through the curtain (that is, through his flesh)— [21] and since we have a great high priest over the house of God, [22] let us draw near with a true heart in full assurance of faith, with our hearts sprinkled clean from an evil conscience and our bodies washed in pure water. [23] Let us hold on to the confession of our hope without wavering, since he who promised is faithful. [24] And let us consider one another in order to provoke love and good works, [25] not neglecting to gather together, as some are in the habit of doing, but encouraging each other, and all the more as you see the day approaching.

THANK YOU FOR YOUR
PROMISE OF ABUNDANT
LIFE AND THAT I GET TO
EXPERIENCE THIS KIND
OF LIFE TODAY.

Russell Kelso Carter

STANDING

ON THE

PROMISES

1. Stand-ing on the prom-is-es   of Christ, my King,   Through e - ter - nal
2. Stand-ing on the prom-is-es   that can - not fail,   When the howl - ing
3. Stand-ing on the prom-is-es   of Christ, the Lord,   Bound to Him   e -
4. Stand-ing on the prom-is-es   I   can - not fall,   Lis - t'ning ev - 'ry

a - ges let His prais - es ring; "Glo-ry in the high-est," I will
storms of doubt and fear as - sail, By the liv-ing Word of God I
ter - nal - ly by love's strong cord, O - ver-com-ing dai-ly with the
mo - ment to the Spir - it's call, Rest-ing in my Sav - ior as my

shout and sing, Stand - ing on the prom - is - es of God.
shall pre - vail, Stand - ing on the prom - is - es of God.
Spir - it's sword, Stand - ing on the prom - is - es of God.
all in all, Stand - ing on the prom - is - es of God.

Chorus

Stand - ing, stand - ing, Stand-ing on the
Stand-ing on the prom - is-es, stand-ing on the prom-is-es,

prom - is-es of God, my Sav - ior; Stand - ing,
Stand-ing on the prom - is-es,

stand - ing, I'm stand-ing on the prom-is-es of God.
stand-ing on the prom - is-es,

HE READS TRUTH

YOU WILL HAVE SUFFERING IN THIS WORLD

ESSAY

When we think about God's promises, we tend to focus on the blessings—forgiveness, mercy, and abundant life. But Jesus promised us something else as well: "You will have suffering in this world" (Jn 16:33). He knows with certainty the pain His people experience in a sin-filled world, and He experienced it Himself.

For many people, God and suffering are not compatible. If God exists, then shouldn't suffering end now? How could a good God allow it? While there are a million ways people have tried to answer this question, we also know that the promise of suffering is not the end of the story; it comes with many more promises of His presence (Jn 16:22, 32), His victory (Jn 16:33), and His provision (Jn 16:23–24). We have Christ, the One who conquered the world, as our promised hope in suffering.

JOHN 16:16–33

SORROW TURNED TO JOY

[16] "In a little while, you will no longer see me; again in a little while, you will see me."

[17] Then some of his disciples said to one another, "What is this he's telling us: 'In a little while, you will not see me; again in a little while, you will see me,' and, 'Because I am going to the Father'?" [18] They said, "What is this he is saying, 'In a little while'? We don't know what he's talking about."

[19] Jesus knew they wanted to ask him, and so he said to them, "Are you asking one another about what I said, 'In a little while, you will not see me; again in a little while, you will see me'? [20] Truly I tell you, you will weep and mourn, but the world will rejoice. You will become sorrowful, but your sorrow will turn to joy. [21] When a woman is in labor, she has pain because her time has come. But when she has given birth to a child, she no longer remembers the suffering because of the joy that a person has been born into the world. [22] So you also have sorrow now. But I will see you again. Your hearts will rejoice, and no one will take away your joy from you.

[23] "In that day you will not ask me anything. Truly I tell you, anything you ask the Father in my name, he will give you. [24] Until now you have asked for nothing in my name. Ask and you will receive, so that your joy may be complete."

JESUS THE VICTOR

[25] "I have spoken these things to you in figures of speech. A time is coming when I will no longer speak to you in figures, but I will tell you plainly about the Father. [26] On that day you will ask in my name, and I am not telling you that I will ask the Father on your behalf. [27] For the Father himself loves you, because you have loved me and have believed that I came from God. [28] I came from the Father and have come into the world. Again, I am leaving the world and going to the Father."

[29] His disciples said, "Look, now you're speaking plainly and not using any figurative language. [30] Now we know that you know everything and

don't need anyone to question you. By this we believe that you came from God."

[31] Jesus responded to them, "Do you now believe? [32] Indeed, an hour is coming, and has come, when each of you will be scattered to his own home, and you will leave me alone. Yet I am not alone, because the Father is with me. [33] I have told you these things so that in me you may have peace. You will have suffering in this world. Be courageous! I have conquered the world."

MATTHEW 10:16–42

PERSECUTIONS PREDICTED

[16] "Look, I'm sending you out like sheep among wolves. Therefore be as shrewd as serpents and as innocent as doves. [17] Beware of them, because they will hand you over to local courts and flog you in their synagogues. [18] You will even be brought before governors and kings because of me, to bear witness to them and to the Gentiles. [19] But when they hand you over, don't worry about how or what you are to speak. For you will be given what to say at that hour, [20] because it isn't you speaking, but the Spirit of your Father is speaking through you.

[21] "Brother will betray brother to death, and a father his child. Children will rise up against parents and have them put to death. [22] You will be hated by everyone because of my name. But the one who endures to the end will be saved. [23] When they persecute you in one town, flee to another. For truly I tell you, you will not have gone through the towns of Israel before the Son of Man comes. [24] A disciple is not above his teacher, or a slave above his master. [25] It is enough for a disciple to become like his teacher and a slave like his master. If they called the head of the house 'Beelzebul,' how much more the members of his household!

FEAR GOD

[26] "Therefore, don't be afraid of them, since there is nothing covered that won't be uncovered and nothing hidden that won't be made known. [27] What I tell you in the dark, speak in the light. What you hear in a whisper, proclaim on the housetops. [28] Don't fear those who kill the body but are not able to kill the soul; rather, fear him who is able to destroy both soul and body in hell. [29] Aren't two sparrows sold for a penny? Yet not one of them falls to the ground without your Father's consent. [30] But even the hairs of

your head have all been counted. [31] So don't be afraid; you are worth more than many sparrows.

ACKNOWLEDGING CHRIST

[32] "Therefore, everyone who will acknowledge me before others, I will also acknowledge him before my Father in heaven. [33] But whoever denies me before others, I will also deny him before my Father in heaven. [34] Don't assume that I came to bring peace on the earth. I did not come to bring peace, but a sword. [35] For I came to turn

> a man against his father,
> a daughter against her mother,
> a daughter-in-law against her
>   mother-in-law;
> [36] and a man's enemies will be
> the members of his household.

[37] The one who loves a father or mother more than me is not worthy of me; the one who loves a son or daughter more than me is not worthy of me. [38] And whoever doesn't take up his cross and follow me is not worthy of me. [39] Anyone who finds his life will lose it, and anyone who loses his life because of me will find it.

A CUP OF COLD WATER

[40] "The one who welcomes you welcomes me, and the one who welcomes me welcomes him who sent me. [41] Anyone who welcomes a prophet because he is a prophet will receive a prophet's reward. And anyone who welcomes a righteous person because he's righteous will receive a righteous person's reward. [42] And whoever gives even a cup of cold water to one of these little ones because he is a disciple, truly I tell you, he will never lose his reward."

2 TIMOTHY 2:8–13

[8] Remember Jesus Christ, risen from the dead and descended from David, according to my gospel, [9] for which I suffer to the point of being bound like a criminal. But the word of God is not bound.

[10] This is why I endure all things for the elect: so that they also may obtain salvation, which is in Christ Jesus, with eternal glory.

[11] This saying is trustworthy:

> For if we died with him,
> we will also live with him;
> [12] if we endure, we will also reign
>   with him;
> if we deny him, he will also deny us;
> [13] if we are faithless, he remains faithful,
> for he cannot deny himself.

THOUGH SUFFERING IS
PROMISED, THANK YOU FOR
GIVING ME YOUR PRESENCE
IN THE MIDST OF IT.

I WILL BE <u>WITH</u> YOU ALWAYS

ESSAY

Jesus was born to fulfill God's promise to send One who would embody the name *Immanuel*, which means "God is with us" (Mt 1:23). He is God incarnate, the living and breathing example of His kingdom to the world. His disciples experienced the tangible presence of God with them, walking and talking in their midst.

Before He returned to heaven, Jesus promised to give a gift that would keep His presence with us always: the Holy Spirit. The Spirit is the way God dwells with us now. The Spirit intercedes for us, guides us according to God's will, and calls us into deeper relationship with God.

MATTHEW 28:16-20

THE GREAT COMMISSION

[16] The eleven disciples traveled to Galilee, to the mountain where Jesus had directed them. [17] When they saw him, they worshiped, but some doubted. [18] Jesus came near and said to them, "All authority has been given to me in heaven and on earth. [19] Go, therefore, and make disciples of all nations, baptizing them in the name of the Father and of the Son and of the Holy Spirit, [20] teaching them to observe everything I have commanded you. And remember, I am with you always, to the end of the age."

JOHN 14:15-17, 25-26

ANOTHER COUNSELOR PROMISED

[15] "If you love me, you will keep my commands. [16] And I will ask the Father, and he will give you another Counselor to be with you forever. [17] He is the Spirit of truth. The world is unable to receive him because it doesn't see him or know him. But you do know him, because he remains with you and will be in you.

…

[25] "I have spoken these things to you while I remain with you.

[26] But the Counselor, the Holy Spirit, whom the Father will send in my name, will teach you all things and remind you of everything I have told you."

ACTS 1:4-8

THE HOLY SPIRIT PROMISED

[4] While he was with them, he commanded them not to leave Jerusalem, but to wait for the Father's promise. "Which," he said, "you have heard me speak about; [5] for John baptized with water, but you will be baptized with the Holy Spirit in a few days."

⁶ So when they had come together, they asked him, "Lord, are you restoring the kingdom to Israel at this time?"

⁷ He said to them, "It is not for you to know times or periods that the Father has set by his own authority. ⁸ But you will receive power when the Holy Spirit has come on you, and you will be my witnesses in Jerusalem, in all Judea and Samaria, and to the ends of the earth."

ROMANS 5:5

This hope will not disappoint us, because God's love has been poured out in our hearts through the Holy Spirit who was given to us.

ROMANS 8:26–27

²⁶ In the same way the Spirit also helps us in our weakness, because we do not know what to pray for as we should, but the Spirit himself intercedes for us with inexpressible groanings. ²⁷ And he who searches our hearts knows the mind of the Spirit, because he intercedes for the saints according to the will of God.

2 THESSALONIANS 2:13–17

¹³ But we ought to thank God always for you, brothers and sisters loved by the Lord, because from the beginning God has chosen you for salvation through sanctification by the Spirit and through belief in the truth. ¹⁴ He called you to this through our gospel, so that you might obtain the glory of our Lord Jesus Christ. ¹⁵ So then, brothers and sisters, stand firm and hold to the traditions you were taught, whether by what we said or what we wrote.

¹⁶ May our Lord Jesus Christ himself and God our Father, who has loved us and given us eternal encouragement and good hope by grace, ¹⁷ encourage your hearts and strengthen you in every good work and word.

THANK YOU FOR YOUR
PROMISED PRESENCE IN
MY LIFE THROUGH THE
HOLY SPIRIT.

GRACE DAY

Take this day to catch up on your reading,
pray, and rest in the presence of the Lord.

LET US
ON ^{TO} THE
^{OF} OUR HOPE
WAVERING,
^{WHO} PROMISED

HOLD CONFESSION WITHOUT SINCE HE IS FAITHFUL.

HEBREWS 10:23

WEEEK

LY

14

DAY

TRUTH

Scripture is God breathed and true. When we memorize it, we carry the good news of Jesus with us wherever we go.

During this reading plan, we are memorizing our key verse. This week we will memorize the second half.

FOR NO MATTER HOW MANY PROMISES GOD HAS MADE, THEY ARE "YES" IN CHRIST. **AND SO THROUGH HIM THE "AMEN" IS SPOKEN BY US TO THE GLORY OF GOD.**

---

2 CORINTHIANS 1:20 NIV

See tips for memorizing Scripture on page 124.

3

<u>WEEK</u>

KINGDOM PROMISES

Scripture's promises about eternity and the kingdom of God remind us that in the new heavens and the new earth, there will be no more tears, no more suffering, no more death, and that we will dwell with the Lord forever. As we await this day when His glory will be fully known, even now the glory of God has already begun to take hold of our world.

I WILL COME AGAIN

ESSAY

The disciples likely had many questions as Jesus prepared them for His imminent departure, and He knew they would not understand all that was soon to take place. So His clear and comforting promise of return was essential: He would indeed come again. In the days following, His disciples remembered this promise as they contemplated all that had taken place during His crucifixion. Despite leaving them physically, He was going to prepare a place for them—one that would be an eternal dwelling once Jesus returned.

All believers on this side of the resurrection and ascension can also take heart that Christ will come again. Because He rose, we will be raised with Him for eternity. Jesus's promise that He will come again points to a future reality, but it also encourages us in the present (1Th 4:18). As members of the kingdom that is both now and not yet, we await His return with sure, steady hope.

JOHN 14:1–4

THE WAY TO THE FATHER

¹ "Don't let your heart be troubled. Believe in God; believe also in me. ² In my Father's house are many rooms. If it were not so, would I have told you that I am going to prepare a place for you? ³ If I go away and prepare a place for you, I will come again and take you to myself, so that where I am you may be also. ⁴ You know the way to where I am going."

1 CORINTHIANS 15:20–24

CHRIST'S RESURRECTION GUARANTEES OURS

²⁰ But as it is, Christ has been raised from the dead, the firstfruits of those who have fallen asleep. ²¹ For since death came through a man, the resurrection of the dead also comes through a man. ²² For just as in Adam all die, so also in Christ all will be made alive.

²³ But each in his own order: Christ, the firstfruits; afterward, at his coming, those who belong to Christ. ²⁴ Then comes the end, when he hands over the kingdom to God the Father, when he abolishes all rule and all authority and power.

1 THESSALONIANS 4:13–18

THE COMFORT OF CHRIST'S COMING

¹³ We do not want you to be uninformed, brothers and sisters, concerning those who are asleep, so that you will not grieve like the rest, who have no hope. ¹⁴ For if we believe that Jesus died and rose again, in the same way, through Jesus, God will bring with him those who have fallen asleep. ¹⁵ For we say this to you by a word from the Lord: We who are still alive at the Lord's coming will certainly not precede those who have fallen asleep. ¹⁶ For the Lord himself will descend from heaven with a shout, with the archangel's voice, and with the trumpet of God, and the dead in Christ will rise first. ¹⁷ Then we who are still alive, who are left, will be caught up together with them in the clouds to meet the Lord in the air, and so we will always be with the Lord. ¹⁸ Therefore encourage one another with these words.

HEBREWS 9:27–28

[27] And just as it is appointed for people to die once—and after this, judgment—

[28] so also Christ, having been offered once to bear the sins of many, will appear a second time, not to bear sin, but to bring salvation to those who are waiting for him.

HEBREWS 10:35–39

[35] So don't throw away your confidence, which has a great reward. [36] For you need endurance, so that after you have done God's will, you may receive what was promised.

[37] For yet in a very little while,
the Coming One will come and not delay.
[38] But my righteous one will live by faith;
and if he draws back,
I have no pleasure in him.

[39] But we are not those who draw back and are destroyed, but those who have faith and are saved.

REVELATION 22:20

He who testifies about these things says, "Yes, I am coming soon."

Amen! Come, Lord Jesus!

Remember to use these prompts as a starting point for your prayer, letting each day's reading shape how you respond to God's promise. Thank Him for how His promises are revealed through Scripture, and ask the Lord for any ways you need help believing these promises.

THANK YOU FOR YOUR
PROMISE TO COME BACK
AGAIN, FOR ME AND ALL
WHO BELIEVE IN YOU.

I WILL SET YOU FREE FROM SIN

ESSAY

In the Gospel of John, Jesus proclaims that "if the Son sets you free, you really will be free" (Jn 8:36). Those listening to Him were undoubtedly confused. In offering freedom, Jesus was implying they were somehow slaves; but they weren't enslaved to anyone, legally or physically. How could they be set free if they weren't in chains?

Scripture is clear that apart from Christ we were once slaves to sin (Jn 8:34) and ruled by death (Rm 6:9). Sin reigned in our bodies (Rm 6:12), and we stood condemned (Rm 8:2). But Jesus went to battle for us against the powers of darkness and came out victorious. His promise of freedom is a timeless one meant for anyone who comes to Christ, but it never depends on our own merit. If the Son frees you, then you are free. While we have indeed been forgiven for eternity, we can experience freedom from the power of sin and the ways of this world in our everyday lives.

JOHN 8:30-36

TRUTH AND FREEDOM

[30] As he was saying these things, many believed in him.

[31] Then Jesus said to the Jews who had believed him, "If you continue in my word, you really are my disciples. [32] You will know the truth, and the truth will set you free."

[33] "We are descendants of Abraham," they answered him, "and we have never been enslaved to anyone. How can you say, 'You will become free'?"

[34] Jesus responded, "Truly I tell you, everyone who commits sin is a slave of sin. [35] A slave does not remain in the household forever, but a son does remain forever. [36] So if the Son sets you free, you really will be free."

ROMANS 6:1-11, 22

THE NEW LIFE IN CHRIST

[1] What should we say then? Should we continue in sin so that grace may multiply? [2] Absolutely not! How can we who died to sin still live in it? [3] Or are you unaware that all of us who were baptized into Christ Jesus were baptized into his death? [4] Therefore we were buried with him by baptism into death, in order that, just as Christ was raised from the dead by the glory of the Father, so we too may walk in newness of life. [5] For if we have been united with him in the likeness of his death, we will certainly also be in the likeness of his resurrection. [6] For we know that our old self was crucified with him so that the body ruled by sin might be rendered powerless so that we may no longer be enslaved to sin, [7] since a person who has died is freed from sin. [8] Now if we died with Christ, we believe that we will also live with him, [9] because we know that Christ, having been raised from the dead, will not die again. Death no longer rules over him. [10] For the death he died, he died to sin once for all time; but the life he lives, he lives to God. [11] So, you too consider yourselves dead to sin and alive to God in Christ Jesus.

…

[22] But now, since you have been set free from sin and have become enslaved to God, you have your fruit, which results in sanctification—and the outcome is eternal life!

ROMANS 8:10-11

[10] Now if Christ is in you, the body is dead because of sin, but the Spirit gives life because of righteousness. [11] And if the Spirit of him who raised Jesus from the dead lives in you, then he who raised Christ from the dead will also bring your mortal bodies to life through his Spirit who lives in you.

HEBREWS 9:11-14

[11] But Christ has appeared as a high priest of the good things that have come. In the greater and more perfect tabernacle not made with hands (that is, not of this creation), [12] he entered the most holy place once for all time, not by the blood of goats and calves, but by his own blood, having obtained eternal redemption. [13] For if the blood of goats and bulls and the ashes of a young cow, sprinkling those who are defiled, sanctify for the purification of the flesh,

[14] how much more will the blood of Christ, who through the eternal Spirit offered himself without blemish to God, cleanse our consciences from dead works so that we can serve the living God?

THANK YOU FOR YOUR
PROMISE TO SET ME FREE
FROM THE POWER OF SIN,
BOTH NOW AND FOREVER.

PROMISES
FOR WHEN...

1
YOU FEEL LONELY.

"And remember, I am with you always, to the end of the age."

MT 28:20

2
YOU ARE WAITING.

I am certain that I will see the LORD's goodness in the land of the living. Wait for the LORD; be strong, and let your heart be courageous. Wait for the LORD.

PS 27:13–14

3
YOU FEEL EXHAUSTED.

"Come to me, all of you who are weary and burdened, and I will give you rest."

MT 11:28

4
YOU FEEL DEFEATED BY SIN.

But God, who is rich in mercy, because of his great love that he had for us, made us alive with Christ even though we were dead in trespasses. You are saved by grace!

EPH 2:4–5

5
YOU FEEL SCARED.

"Peace I leave with you. My peace I give to you. I do not give to you as the world gives. Don't let your heart be troubled or fearful."

JN 14:27

6
YOU FEEL HOPELESS.

Because of the LORD's faithful love we do not perish, for his mercies never end. They are new every morning; great is your faithfulness!

LM 3:22–23

7
YOU FEEL ANXIOUS.

"Consider the birds of the sky: They don't sow or reap or gather into barns, yet your heavenly Father feeds them. Aren't you worth more than they? Can any of you add one moment to his life span by worrying?...So don't worry, saying, 'What will we eat?' or 'What will we drink?' or 'What will we wear?' For the Gentiles eagerly seek all these things, and your heavenly Father knows that you need them. But seek first the kingdom of God and his righteousness, and all these things will be provided for you."

MT 6:26–27, 31–33

8
YOU FEEL SAD.

Look, God's dwelling is with humanity, and he will live with them. They will be his peoples, and God himself will be with them and will be their God. He will wipe away every tear from their eyes. Death will be no more; grief, crying, and pain will be no more, because the previous things have passed away.

RV 21:3–4

9
YOU FEEL DISAPPOINTED.

And not only that, but we also boast in our afflictions, because we know that affliction produces endurance, endurance produces proven character, and proven character produces hope. This hope will not disappoint us, because God's love has been poured out in our hearts through the Holy Spirit who was given to us.

RM 5:3–5

I WILL PROVIDE FOR YOU

ESSAY

Trusting God's promise of provision can be more difficult in practice than believing it on principle. Yet since the beginning, God has been our provider, giving us the air in our lungs and the food in our stomachs (Gn 1:29; 2:7). The first temptation showed us just how quickly we doubt God as our good provider. The lie that began at the fall has governed much of our behavior ever since.

During His time on earth, Jesus modeled what it looks like to depend on God for all we need, while actively seeking Him first and foremost. He shows us how the worries and cares of this world can be replaced by contentment and abundance, trusting God knows our needs best. He spoke truth to break the devil's ancient yet persistent lie, declaring that whatever we may build for ourselves on earth will crumble in the end; only that which is eternal—what is stored up in heaven—will last (Mt 6:19–20). Therefore, even as we await the provision of eternity with Christ, we trust that in His presence, we lack nothing.

MATTHEW 6:25-34

[25] "Therefore I tell you: Don't worry about your life, what you will eat or what you will drink; or about your body, what you will wear. Isn't life more than food and the body more than clothing? [26] Consider the birds of the sky: They don't sow or reap or gather into barns, yet your heavenly Father feeds them. Aren't you worth more than they? [27] Can any of you add one moment to his life span by worrying? [28] And why do you worry about clothes? Observe how the wildflowers of the field grow: They don't labor or spin thread. [29] Yet I tell you that not even Solomon in all his splendor was adorned like one of these. [30] If that's how God clothes the grass of the field, which is here today and thrown into the furnace tomorrow, won't he do much more for you—you of little faith? [31] So don't worry, saying, 'What will we eat?' or 'What will we drink?' or 'What will we wear?' [32] For the Gentiles eagerly seek all these things, and your heavenly Father knows that you need them. [33] But seek first the kingdom of God and his righteousness, and all these things will be provided for you. [34] Therefore don't worry about tomorrow, because tomorrow will worry about itself. Each day has enough trouble of its own."

MATTHEW 7:7-11

ASK, SEARCH, KNOCK

[7] "Ask, and it will be given to you. Seek, and you will find. Knock, and the door will be opened to you. [8] For everyone who asks receives, and the one who seeks finds, and to the one who knocks, the door will be opened. [9] Who among you, if his son asks him for bread, will give him a stone? [10] Or if he asks for a fish, will give him a snake?

[11] If you then, who are evil, know how to give good gifts to your children, how much more will your Father in heaven give good things to those who ask him."

PHILIPPIANS 4:10–20

APPRECIATION OF SUPPORT

[10] I rejoiced in the Lord greatly because once again you renewed your care for me. You were, in fact, concerned about me but lacked the opportunity to show it. [11] I don't say this out of need, for I have learned to be content in whatever circumstances I find myself. [12] I know how to make do with little, and I know how to make do with a lot. In any and all circumstances I have learned the secret of being content—whether well fed or hungry, whether in abundance or in need. [13] I am able to do all things through him who strengthens me. [14] Still, you did well by partnering with me in my hardship.

[15] And you Philippians know that in the early days of the gospel, when I left Macedonia, no church shared with me in the matter of giving and receiving except you alone. [16] For even in Thessalonica you sent gifts for my need several times. [17] Not that I seek the gift, but I seek the profit that is increasing to your account. [18] But I have received everything in full, and I have an abundance. I am fully supplied, having received from Epaphroditus what you provided—a fragrant offering, an acceptable sacrifice, pleasing to God. [19] And my God will supply all your needs according to his riches in glory in Christ Jesus. [20] Now to our God and Father be glory forever and ever. Amen.

PSALM 23

THE GOOD SHEPHERD

A psalm of David.

[1] The LORD is my shepherd;
I have what I need.
[2] He lets me lie down in green pastures;
he leads me beside quiet waters.
[3] He renews my life;
he leads me along the right paths
for his name's sake.
[4] Even when I go through the darkest valley,
I fear no danger,
for you are with me;
your rod and your staff—they comfort me.

[5] You prepare a table before me
in the presence of my enemies;
you anoint my head with oil;
my cup overflows.
[6] Only goodness and faithful love will
pursue me
all the days of my life,
and I will dwell in the house of the LORD
as long as I live.

JAMES 1:17

Every good and perfect gift is from above, coming down from the Father of lights, who does not change like shifting shadows.

THANK YOU FOR YOUR
PROMISE TO PROVIDE ALL
THAT I NEED.

I WILL GIVE YOU ETERNAL LIFE

ESSAY

The promise of eternal life hinges on Jesus being the resurrection and life (Jn 11:25). If He had not been more powerful than death, we would have no hope. But it can be hard to imagine a world where believers are raised in glory and power, and where their natural, earthly bodies have been transformed (1Co 15:40, 42–44). The promise of a glorious resurrection stands in contrast to just about everything that we experience on a day-to-day basis here on earth.

Living with this promise in view is an example of what it looks like to experience the already-and-not-yet nature of God's kingdom. Amidst the death and decay of our present world, believers get to experience the glory of having the Spirit of God reside within us (Eph 1:14), reminding us of the perfect communion we'll get to experience with God forever in the new heaven and new earth. Even though the fullness of eternal life may seem like a far-off reality, because of Christ, it is our guarantee.

JOHN 3:14-17

[14] "Just as Moses lifted up the snake in the wilderness, so the Son of Man must be lifted up, [15] so that everyone who believes in him may have eternal life. [16] For God loved the world in this way: He gave his one and only Son, so that everyone who believes in him will not perish but have eternal life. [17] For God did not send his Son into the world to condemn the world, but to save the world through him."

JOHN 11:17-27

THE RESURRECTION AND THE LIFE

[17] When Jesus arrived, he found that Lazarus had already been in the tomb four days. [18] Bethany was near Jerusalem (less than two miles away). [19] Many of the Jews had come to Martha and Mary to comfort them about their brother.

[20] As soon as Martha heard that Jesus was coming, she went to meet him, but Mary remained seated in the house. [21] Then Martha said to Jesus, "Lord, if you had been here, my brother wouldn't have died. [22] Yet even now I know that whatever you ask from God, God will give you."

[23] "Your brother will rise again," Jesus told her.

[24] Martha said to him, "I know that he will rise again in the resurrection at the last day."

[25] Jesus said to her, "I am the resurrection and the life. The one who believes in me, even if he dies, will live. [26] Everyone who lives and believes in me will never die. Do you believe this?"

[27] "Yes, Lord," she told him, "I believe you are the Messiah, the Son of God, who comes into the world."

JOHN 17:3

"This is eternal life: that they may know you, the only true God, and the one you have sent—Jesus Christ."

You reveal the path of life to me;
in your presence is abundant joy;

at your right hand are eternal pleasures.

1 CORINTHIANS 15:50-58

VICTORIOUS RESURRECTION

[50] What I am saying, brothers and sisters, is this: Flesh and blood cannot inherit the kingdom of God, nor can corruption inherit incorruption. [51] Listen, I am telling you a mystery: We will not all fall asleep, but we will all be changed, [52] in a moment, in the twinkling of an eye, at the last trumpet. For the trumpet will sound, and the dead will be raised incorruptible, and we will be changed. [53] For this corruptible body must be clothed with incorruptibility, and this mortal body must be clothed with immortality. [54] When this corruptible body is clothed with incorruptibility, and this mortal body is clothed with immortality, then the saying that is written will take place:

Death has been swallowed up in victory.
[55] Where, death, is your victory?
Where, death, is your sting?

[56] The sting of death is sin, and the power of sin is the law. [57] But thanks be to God, who gives us the victory through our Lord Jesus Christ!

[58] Therefore, my dear brothers and sisters, be steadfast, immovable, always excelling in the Lord's work, because you know that your labor in the Lord is not in vain.

ROMANS 6:23

For the wages of sin is death, but the gift of God is eternal life in Christ Jesus our Lord.

1 JOHN 2:24-25

REMAINING WITH GOD

[24] What you have heard from the beginning is to remain in you. If what you have heard from the beginning remains in you, then you will remain in the Son and in the Father. [25] And this is the promise that he himself made to us: eternal life.

1 PETER 1:3-9

[3] Blessed be the God and Father of our Lord Jesus Christ. Because of his great mercy he has given us new birth into a living hope through the resurrection of Jesus Christ from the dead [4] and into an inheritance that is imperishable, undefiled, and unfading, kept in heaven for you. [5] You are being guarded by God's power through faith for a salvation that is ready to be revealed in the last time. [6] You rejoice in this, even though now for a short time, if necessary, you suffer grief in various trials [7] so that the proven character of your faith—more valuable than gold which, though perishable, is refined by fire—may result in praise, glory, and honor at the revelation of Jesus Christ. [8] Though you have not seen him, you love him; though not seeing him now, you believe in him, and you rejoice with inexpressible and glorious joy, [9] because you are receiving the goal of your faith, the salvation of your souls.

THANK YOU FOR YOUR
PROMISE OF ETERNAL LIFE
THAT I CAN HOPE IN DESPITE
THE DEATH AND DECAY OF
THIS PRESENT WORLD.

I WILL MAKE EVERYTHING NEW

ESSAY

The heartache and sorrow of this world is enough to break us, and can often feel like the inevitable end. And though we may look out and see a world twisted and marred by sin, God has promised to make everything new. How this will happen is largely a mystery, and this is why God's promise to make all things new just might be the one that requires the greatest amount of faith.

Through the cross, God has made a way for His goodness to permeate our world and overtake the curse of sin. He has promised to make all things new, including the brokenness we see in and around us. We glimpse this final outcome as Revelation 21:3–4 says, "grief, crying, and pain will be no more." We trust that this will be reality one day because of the One who made this promise, and we seek Him to understand how we can bring pieces of that promise to our world through our loving action now.

REVELATION 21:1-7

[1] Then I saw a new heaven and a new earth; for the first heaven and the first earth had passed away, and the sea was no more. [2] I also saw the holy city, the new Jerusalem, coming down out of heaven from God, prepared like a bride adorned for her husband.

[3] Then I heard a loud voice from the throne: Look, God's dwelling is with humanity, and he will live with them. They will be his peoples, and God himself will be with them and will be their God. [4] He will wipe away every tear from their eyes. Death will be no more; grief, crying, and pain will be no more, because the previous things have passed away.

[5] Then the one seated on the throne said, "Look, I am making everything new." He also said, "Write, because these words are faithful and true." [6] Then he said to me, "It is done! I am the Alpha and the Omega, the beginning and the end. I will freely give to the thirsty from the spring of the water of life. [7] The one who conquers will inherit these things, and I will be his God, and he will be my son."

ISAIAH 65:17-25

A NEW CREATION

[17] "For I will create new heavens and a new earth;
the past events will not be remembered or come to mind.
[18] Then be glad and rejoice forever
in what I am creating;
for I will create Jerusalem to be a joy
and its people to be a delight.
[19] I will rejoice in Jerusalem
and be glad in my people.
The sound of weeping and crying
will no longer be heard in her.
[20] In her, a nursing infant will no longer live
only a few days,
or an old man not live out his days.
Indeed, the one who dies at a hundred years old
will be mourned as a young man,

and the one who misses a hundred years
will be considered cursed.
²¹ People will build houses and live in them;
they will plant vineyards and eat their fruit.
²² They will not build and others live in them;
they will not plant and others eat.

For my people's lives will be
like the lifetime of a tree.
My chosen ones will fully enjoy
the work of their hands.

²³ They will not labor without success
or bear children destined for disaster,
for they will be a people blessed by the Lord
along with their descendants.
²⁴ Even before they call, I will answer;
while they are still speaking, I will hear.
²⁵ The wolf and the lamb will feed together,
and the lion will eat straw like cattle,
but the serpent's food will be dust!
They will not do what is evil or destroy
on my entire holy mountain,"
says the LORD.

HEBREWS 13:14

For we do not have an enduring city here; instead, we seek the one
to come.

1 CORINTHIANS 2:6–12

SPIRITUAL WISDOM

⁶ We do, however, speak a wisdom among the mature, but not a wisdom
of this age, or of the rulers of this age, who are coming to nothing. ⁷ On
the contrary, we speak God's hidden wisdom in a mystery, a wisdom God
predestined before the ages for our glory. ⁸ None of the rulers of this age
knew this wisdom, because if they had known it, they would not have
crucified the Lord of glory. ⁹ But as it is written,

What no eye has seen, no ear has heard,
and no human heart has conceived—
God has prepared these things for those who love him.

[10] Now God has revealed these things to us by the Spirit, since the Spirit searches everything, even the depths of God. [11] For who knows a person's thoughts except his spirit within him? In the same way, no one knows the thoughts of God except the Spirit of God. [12] Now we have not received the spirit of the world, but the Spirit who comes from God, so that we may understand what has been freely given to us by God.

THANK YOU FOR YOUR
PROMISE TO MAKE ALL
THINGS NEW.

GRACE DAY

Take this day to catch up on your reading,
pray, and rest in the presence of the Lord.

SO DON'T AWAY YOUR WHICH HAS A FOR YOU NEED SO THAT AFTER GOD'S WILL, RECEIVE WHAT

THROW
CONFIDENCE,
GREAT REWARD.
ENDURANCE,
YOU HAVE DONE
YOU MAY
WAS PROMISED.

HEBREWS 10:35–36

WEEKLY

21

DAY

TRUTH

Scripture is God breathed and true. When we memorize it, we carry the good news of Jesus with us wherever we go.

For this reading plan, we have been memorizing our key verse for this plan. This week, we are committing the entire verse to memory.

FOR NO MATTER HOW MANY PROMISES GOD HAS MADE, THEY ARE "YES" IN CHRIST. AND SO THROUGH HIM THE "AMEN" IS SPOKEN BY US TO THE GLORY OF GOD.

2 CORINTHIANS 1:20 NIV

See tips for memorizing Scripture on page 124.

BENEDICTION

GOD MAKES A PROMISE;
FAITH BELIEVES IT;
HOPE ANTICIPATES IT;
AND PATIENCE QUIETLY
AWAITS IT.

D. L. MOODY

Tips for Memorizing Scripture

At He Reads Truth, we believe Scripture memorization is an important discipline in your walk with God. Committing God's Word to memory means we carry it with us and we can minister to others wherever we go. As you approach the Weekly Truth verse in this book, try these memorization tips to see which techniques work best for you.

STUDY IT

Study the passage in its biblical context, and ask yourself a few questions before you begin to memorize it: What does this passage say? What does it mean? How would I say this in my own words? What does it teach me about God? Understanding what the passage means helps you know why it is important to carry it with you wherever you go.

Break the passage into smaller sections, memorizing a phrase at a time.

PRAY IT

Use the passage you are memorizing as a prompt for prayer.

WRITE IT

Dedicate a notebook to Scripture memorization, and write the passage over and over again.

Diagram the passage after you write it out. Place a square around the verbs, underline the nouns, and circle any adjectives or adverbs. Say the passage aloud several times, emphasizing the verbs as you repeat it. Then do the same thing again with the nouns, then the adjectives and adverbs.

Write out the first letter of each word in the passage somewhere you can reference it throughout the week as you work on your memorization.

Use a whiteboard to write out the passage. Erase a few words at a time as you continue to repeat it aloud. Keep erasing parts of the passage until you have it all committed to memory.

CREATE

If you can, make up a tune for the passage to sing as you go about your day, or try singing it to the tune of a favorite song.

Use hand signals or signs to come up with associations for each word or phrase, and repeat the movements as you practice.

SAY IT

Repeat the passage out loud to yourself as you are going through the rhythm of your day—getting ready, pouring your coffee, waiting in traffic, or making dinner.

Listen to the passage read aloud to you.

Record a voice memo on your phone, and listen to it throughout the day, or play it on an audio Bible.

SHARE IT

Memorize the passage with a friend, family member, or mentor. Spontaneously challenge each other to recite the passage, or pick a time to review your passage and practice saying it from memory together.

Send the passage as an encouraging text to a friend, testing yourself as you type to see how much you have memorized so far.

KEEP AT IT

Set reminders on your phone to prompt you to practice your passage.

Keep a stack of note cards with Scripture you are memorizing by your bed. Practice reciting what you've memorized previously before you go to sleep, ending with the passages you are currently learning. If you wake up in the middle of the night, review them again instead of grabbing your phone. Read them out loud before you get out of bed in the morning.

CSB BOOK ABBREVIATIONS

OLD TESTAMENT

GN Genesis

EX Exodus

LV Leviticus

NM Numbers

DT Deuteronomy

JOS Joshua

JDG Judges

RU Ruth

1SM 1 Samuel

2SM 2 Samuel

1KG 1 Kings

2KG 2 Kings

1CH 1 Chronicles

2CH 2 Chronicles

EZR Ezra

NEH Nehemiah

EST Esther

JB Job

PS Psalms

PR Proverbs

EC Ecclesiastes

SG Song of Solomon

IS Isaiah

JR Jeremiah

LM Lamentations

EZK Ezekiel

DN Daniel

HS Hosea

JL Joel

AM Amos

OB Obadiah

JNH Jonah

MC Micah

NAH Nahum

HAB Habakkuk

ZPH Zephaniah

HG Haggai

ZCH Zechariah

MAL Malachi

NEW TESTAMENT

MT Matthew

MK Mark

LK Luke

JN John

AC Acts

RM Romans

1CO 1 Corinthians

2CO 2 Corinthians

GL Galatians

EPH Ephesians

PHP Philippians

COL Colossians

1TH 1 Thessalonians

2TH 2 Thessalonians

1TM 1 Timothy

2TM 2 Timothy

TI Titus

PHM Philemon

HEB Hebrews

JMS James

1PT 1 Peter

2PT 2 Peter

1JN 1 John

2JN 2 John

3JN 3 John

JD Jude

RV Revelation

BIBLIOGRAPHY   Moody, D. L. *Pleasure and Profit in Bible Study*. Chicago: Fleming H. Revell Company, 1895.

SHOP THE
HE READS TRUTH
ONLINE BOOKSTORE

RESOURCES TO HELP YOU READ

AND UNDERSTAND GOD'S WORD

Our Online Bookstore is stocked with Daily Reading Guides and supporting resources, available for you to start whenever you're ready. The collection includes guides on books of the Bible, topics that matter, and seasons of the Church calendar. Read on your own, with your church, or with your friends or family.

IN OUR ONLINE BOOKSTORE YOU'LL FIND

DAILY READING GUIDES   Each of our Daily Reading Guides is available for you to start reading on your own or with a group, whenever you are ready.

BIBLES   Shop our collection of thoughtfully and artfully designed Bibles.

OTHER RESOURCES   Whether you're looking for books to point your kids toward God through His Word or a curated Bible reading gift set, we've got just the thing.

SHOP NOW!
SHOPHEREADSTRUTH.COM

You just spent 21 days in the Word of God.

My favorite day of this reading plan:

How did I find delight in God's Word?

One thing I learned about God:

What was God doing in my life during this study?

What did I learn that I want to share with someone else?

A specific passage or verse that encouraged me:

A specific passage or verse that challenged and convicted me: